Author:

Steve Parker has a First Class Honours BSc, is a Senior Scientific Fellow of the Zoological Society, worked at London's Natural History Museum and several publishers, and is now a full-time science and nature author. He has written or contributed to more than 300 books and websites, including 70-plus on dinosaurs and other prehistoric life.

Series creator:

David Salariya was born in Dundee, Scotland. He has illustrated a wide range of books and has created and designed many new series for publishers in the UK and overseas. David established The Salariya Book Company in 1989. He lives in Brighton with his wife, illustrator Shirley Willis, and their son Jonathan.

Artists:

Caroline Romanet
Bryan Beach

Editor:

Jacqueline Ford

Published in Great Britain in MMXVIII by Book House, an imprint of
The Salariya Book Company Ltd
25 Marlborough Place, Brighton BN1 1UB
www.salariya.com

HB ISBN: 978-1-912006-45-8
PB ISBN: 978-1-912006-98-4

SCRIBO   BOOK HOUSE   SCRIBBLERS

© The Salariya Book Company Ltd MMXVIII

1 3 5 7 9 8 6 4 2

A CIP catalogue record for this book is available from the British Library.

Printed and bound in China.

Visit
www.salariya.com
for our online catalogue and **free** fun stuff.

The Science of Killer Dinosaurs

The Blood-Curdling Truth About T. rex and other Theropods

Written by
Steve Parker

Illustrated by
Caroline Romanet

BOOK HOUSE
a SALARIYA imprint

Contents

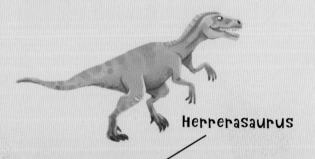

Herrerasaurus

Dilophosaurus

| Triassic: 252-201 mya | Jurassic: 201-145 mya |

Mya = Million years ago

Introduction

The Age of Dinosaurs lasted for most of the Mesozoic era (meaning 'Middle Life'), from 252 to 65 million years ago. And what an age it was! Among those huge reptiles were the biggest, strongest, fiercest killers ever to walk the Earth. They had to be, because their victims were even more massive, some as big as houses! All of these dinosaur predators belonged to the group called theropods, which means 'beast feet'. But not all theropods were huge. Some were tiny, smaller than a pet cat. Yet they were also extremely ferocious and deadly for their size.

Hundreds of kinds of theropods came and went through the Age of Dinosaurs. They lived all over the world. They hunted a wide variety of prey, from little bugs and worms, to their closest dinosaur cousins, the immense, long-necked, long-tailed sauropods. The following pages explain the science behind the most fearsome, deadly predators ever to prowl our planet.

Giganotosaurus

Cretaceous: 145-65 mya

Teeth

All killer dinosaurs had long, pointed teeth. But these differed in details. Some were wide and stout, like bananas. Others were narrow with sharp edges, like knife blades. Some had ridges that were serrated like saws. Daspletosaurus, 9 m (30 ft) in length, had about 70 long teeth that were not especially sharp, but were thick and strong for tearing.

Tarbosaurus had all the great killer features, from sharp eyesight to lethal claws. It stalked Asia at the same time that its close cousin, Tyrannosaurus, prowled North America.

Key features

Today's biggest land killers are grizzly bears, over 3 metres (10 feet) in length and weighing around 500 kilograms (half a tonne). Tigers and lions are almost as large. But all these are puny compared to the greatest killer dinosaurs, who were five times longer and over 20 times heavier! Those dinosaurs had similar hunting weapons – sharp teeth, long claws, keen eyesight and other senses, and fast, agile movements. We know this because dinosaur teeth, claws, and bones have been preserved as fossils. They tell us how those ferocious hunters stalked, attacked, killed and ate their prey.

Claws

Theropods had long, curved toe claws, and similar but smaller finger claws. Some used their claws to tear and wound prey so it bled to death. Others held their victim with their claws while ripping it apart with their teeth. Utahraptor had an extra large claw on its second toe that it could flick around in a lethal swipe.

Fossils show that theropod bones were not solid all the way through. They had spaces inside, and many of these spaces were filled with air. This made the bones much lighter in weight, yet still strong. Birds have very similar hollow bones, which is part of the evidence that birds evolved from theropod dinosaurs.

Senses

Fossil skull bones show that predatory dinosaurs had excellent senses. Their eyes faced forward, to see details and judge distances when leaping on prey. Among the biggest eyes, compared to body size, were those of little Sinornithoides, which was just 1 m (3 ft) long.

Limbs

Many dinosaurs, especially plant eaters, walked on all four legs. But hunters moved on their rear limbs only, which were long with strong muscles. In particular, the long shins and feet were suited to speedy sprints after prey. At 10 m (32 ft) in length, Yangchuanosaurus could probably race after and catch almost any victim of its time.

The first killers

The first dinosaurs appeared more than 235 million years ago. They were not especially huge, but they were already deadly hunters. One of the earliest was Herrerasaurus, which lived 231 million years ago in what is now Argentina, South America. It grew to 4 m (13 ft) in length – although almost half of this was its long, tapering tail – and it weighed up to 300 kg (660 pounds). With its long snout, a mouthful of pointy teeth, sharp-clawed hands, and the ability to run on its powerful rear legs, it already had the shape and characteristics of the killers to come.

Small beginnings

Fossils have not yet been found to show exactly where and when dinosaurs first appeared. But fossils of other reptiles suggest theropods evolved from smaller creatures similar to Euparkeria. This reptile lived in South Africa, was only 60 cm (23 in) long, and moved mainly on all fours. Yet it had sharp teeth and a killing lifestyle – like theropods.

I evolved from something like that?!

Skull and teeth

Compared to later killers, Herrerasaurus had a small head and a long, narrow skull for its body size. The jaws were lined with up to 80 large serrated teeth. As in most theropods, the teeth were recurved – hook-shaped and pointing backwards. This prevented struggling prey from slipping out of its mouth.

Hmm, time to cut my toenails.

What did Herrerasaurus eat? Not birds or mammals – they hadn't evolved yet. Likely prey included plant-eating reptiles and large bugs and worms.

Hands and feet

Herrersaurus's hand had five fingers, although the fourth and fifth were very small. The foot had five toes, which, like the five fingers, was a 'primitive' feature. This does not mean outdated or no good, just that it evolved early in the group's history. Most later theropods had fewer fingers and toes.

Famous fossil finds

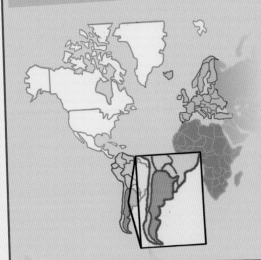

(Your-name-here)-saurus! Dinosaurs and other animals are sometimes named after their discoverers. Herrerasaurus means 'Herrera's lizard'. It was named in 1963 after Andean farmer and goat keeper Victorino Herrera, who liked to look for fossils as he worked.

q

Among reptiles, dinosaurs were not alone in having show-off crests and flaps. Some lizards today have them, like anoles and horned lizards. Usually they are bigger in the male, to attract females and warn off rival males.

Getting bigger!

D inosaurs began during the first period (time span) of the Mesozoic era – the Triassic, 252 to 201 million years ago. As the next period – the Jurassic – began, dinosaurs were becoming more common around the world, and also bigger. One of the first large theropods was Dilophosaurus. Its fossils are about 190 million years old and found in Arizona, USA. Dilophosaurus reached 400 kg (880 lb) in weight and was 7 m (23 ft) long – around the same as today's biggest crocodiles.

Cool killer

Cryolophosaurus was similar in size to Dilophosaurus, and was also from the Early Jurassic. It too had a bony head crest, shaped like a seashell, probably for showing off. But Cryolophosaurus lived far from Arizona – in Antarctica! However, this great continent was further north then, and much warmer. This shows how bigger killers were spreading around the world.

It's a race!

One way for prey to defend against predators is to become gradually bigger over the long time periods of evolution. However, predators might then also evolve into larger sizes. Dilophosaurus may have been part of this 'size race' as it tackled victims such as Ammosaurus, which was up to 5 m (16 ft) long itself.

Fascinating fact

Dilophosaurus is often shown with a neck frill of spines folding out bright skin. This was how it looked in the movie *Jurassic Park* (1993). But there's no evidence for a frill. The movie-makers made it up!

One fossil of Dilophosaurus had numerous bone injuries, including a broken arm, and damaged fingers and shoulder. Some of these showed signs of healing, so it seems the killer managed to recover despite the pain.

Head crests

Dilophosaurus had two bony crests, each like half a dinner plate, on its head. Were they weapons, like a ram's horns, to head-butt prey, enemies, or even each other? The bone was thin and weak so that's unlikely. They were probably for show or display. Maybe covered with bright-coloured skin and scales, they impressed mates and frightened rivals.

My crest's better than yours.

Dream on.

Jurassic giant-killers

Some of the most complete dinosaur fossils ever found belong to Allosaurus. A specimen in Montana is almost entirely complete. It's known as 'Big Al.'

Towards the end of the Jurassic period, which ended 145 million years ago, some dinosaurs became enormous. Plant-eating sauropods like Diplodocus and Brachiosaurus, more than 20 m (65 ft) long and weighing tens of tonnes, plodded and munched their way around North America. Stalking them was one of the biggest killers of the time – Allosaurus, 11 m (36 ft) in length and 2 tonnes in weight. Hundreds of Allosaurus fossils of different sizes and ages have been found, many from the famous Cleveland-Lloyd Dinosaur Quarry in Utah, USA.

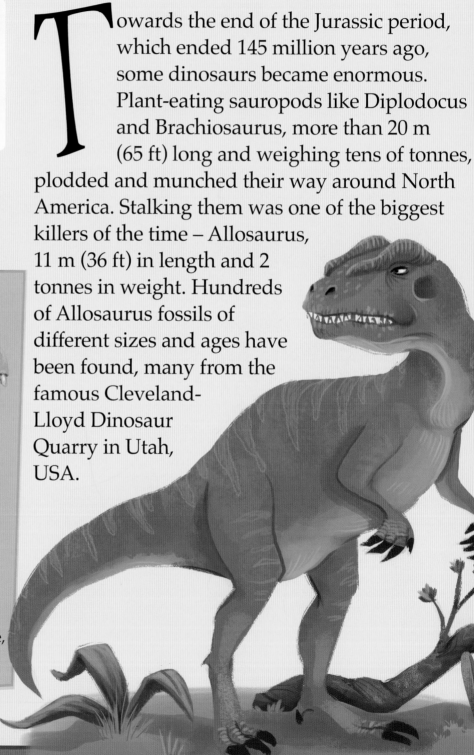

Horn-head

Similar to Allosaurus, and also from the Late Jurassic, was Ceratosaurus. Its remains come from North America, Europe and Africa. It had a thin rounded 'horn' on its nose and two narrower horns over its eyes. It was slightly smaller than Allosaurus, but in Europe, it was still one of the biggest predators of its time.

Too big to tackle?

Some sets of Allosaurus fossils were found close together in the same place. Does this mean they hunted together in a pack, like today's lions or wolves, to bring down their colossal meal? Or perhaps they simply gathered together to scavenge at the massive carcasses of sauropods that had died of old age or sickness.

With so many and varied fossils of Allosaurus, some experts suggest there were several kinds or species, such as A. fragilis, A. europaeus and A. lucasi. Others say it's just normal variation to do with age, females and males, and different locations.

Changing names

Allosaurus was named in 1877 by the great fossil hunter Othniel Charles Marsh. In the 1920s another expert, Charles Gilmore, decided Allosaurus was the same as another dinosaur, Antrodemus, named earlier in 1873, so the name Allosaurus should be dropped. In 1976 yet another expert, James Madsen, said the identification of Antrodemus was based on not enough fossils, so it should be dropped instead, and Allosaurus used again!

~~Antrodemus~~
Allosaurus

Can you believe it?

During its teenage years, Allosaurus grew at an astonishing rate – up to 0.5 kg (1 lb.) each day! That's 30 times more than a human teenager. As it reached its twenties, this rate slowed. But, unlike humans, it never quite stopped growing.

I think I've got growing pains...

13

How big?

The enormous claw Bill Walker found was more than 30 cm (11 in) around its outer edge, and would have been on the first finger of Baryonyx. An early idea was that it could be a hook to catch and lift fish out of the water. This is similar to the pole and hook known as a gaff, used by human anglers to hoist heavy fish from the water.

Hook 'n' claw

In 1983 plumber and part-time fossil hunter Bill Walker was poking around Smokejacks Pit clay quarry in Surrey, England. He found a strange-shaped lump of rock, bashed it with his hammer, and it split to reveal a massive curved claw! He called in the experts, who dug out the rest of the fossils and put them together to recreate the form of Baryonyx, a fierce theropod 8 m (26 ft) long and weighing 1.5 tonnes. It lived in the Early Cretaceous period, 130 million years ago. The *Jaws* shark movies were popular at the time, so Baryonyx soon became known as 'Claws'.

Duh-nuh... duh-nuh... duh-nuh, duh-nuh, duh-nuh, duh-nuh!

Baryonyx did not eat only fish. In addition to the fish scales found in the stomach region of the fossil remains, there were also some bones of a young plant-eating dinosaur, Iguanodon.

A fishy place

Fossils found with Baryonyx showed that its habitat had plentiful water in rivers, streams, lakes and pools. This was ideal for a fish-eater. Baryonyx's long, slim jaws and small teeth were also similar in shape to the large crocodile today called the gharial, which is a fish-catching specialist.

Survival tactics

Other theropod dinosaurs lived in the area, as well as crocodiles, which would have competed with Baryonyx for water-dwelling prey. Baryonyx's thumb claws would have made awesome defensive weapons against its enemies.

Dino-fisher

The fossils of Baryonyx gave experts the first clues that a theropod dinosaur could be adapted to eat fish, which is known as piscivory (rather than carnivory, or eating meaty flesh). More evidence came from fish scales preserved in the remains of Baryonyx where its stomach would have been.

Baryonyx's fish-catching features puzzled scientists for a while. But they soon recognised similarities to other finds, such as Spinosaurus and Suchomimus.

Fierce family

Tyrannosaurs were a large, long-lived family of killers. Early members were small and slim, such as Guanlong from the Late Jurassic, 155 million years ago, which was about 3 m (10 ft) long but stood knee-high to a human. Eotyrannus, about as tall as a human, lived 130 million years ago in England. Dilong, from 125 million years ago, was knee-high to a human, and had feathers.

Feathered foes

I t might seem strange to picture huge, deadly killer dinosaurs covered in wispy, maybe colourful feathers. But since the 1996 discovery of fossil feathers on the small theropod Sinosauropteryx, it's clear many dinosaurs had them. Some feathers were in fossils already examined and named, but experts missed them, and they were only noticed after more studies. Others are newer discoveries, like the biggest killer known so far with direct fossil evidence for feathers – Yutyrannus. Living 125 million years ago in China, this early cousin of the great Tyrannosaurus was 9 m (30 ft) long and weighed around 1.5 tonnes.

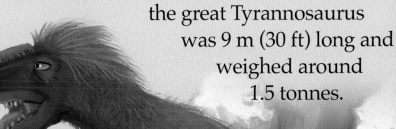

Hairy feathers

Yutyrannus's feathers were not stiff and branched, like a modern bird's flight feathers. They were long, unbranched and flexible, more like hairs, some reaching 20 cm (8 inches) in length. Different fossil specimens of Yutyrannus had them on various parts of the body including the neck, arm, hip, leg and tail.

Yutyrannus was an early member of the tyrannosaurs. But this does not mean it was the ancestor of the famous T. rex. More likely, it was on a side branch of the family tree.

Why feathers?

The feathers of Yutyrannus were totally unsuited for flight – and this predator weighed over 1 tonne! They may have been like a living duvet to keep out the cold, since the habitat at the time had a cool climate. Another reason for Yutyrannus's feathers could have been for appearance, such as dull colours for camouflage, or bright colours for display.

I feel like trying out a new colour...

Can you believe it?

Scientists are not sure exactly where Yutyrannus fossils were found. They were dug up in secret by people hired by fossil dealers, mainly to sell and make money, rather than advance scientific knowledge. In fact, this occurs often.

17

Preen-clean

Microraptor's feathers were up to 20 cm (8 in) long on its arms and 15 cm (6 in) long on its legs. Each had a central stalk or quill with side vanes, similar to the flight feathers of modern birds. Microraptor probably spent a lot of time combing, cleaning and preening them with its teeth and claws, like birds today.

Compared to its tiny body, Microraptor's feathers were long. They would have made running quite difficult, especially through plants and undergrowth.

Tiny terrors

Not all killer dinosaurs were as big as trucks with teeth the size of carving knives. There were little theropods too, that were also deadly. They hunted bugs, worms, and small reptiles such as lizards. One of the smallest and strangest of these mini-predators was Microraptor, from 120 million years ago in what is now China. It was only about 75 to 100 cm (30 to 40 in) long and weighed around 1 kg (2 lb.). It also had very unusual features not found in other dinosaurs, or even other vertebrates (animals with a backbone): four feathered limbs – or were they wings?

What were their feathers for?

Microraptor's feathers were very similar to those of today's birds, so they were probably used for flight. They could have had other uses too, such as for a colourful display, and keeping warm in cool conditions. Maybe Microraptor shed or moulted them to grow new ones, in the same way that birds do.

Micro-flier

Careful study of Microraptor's shoulder, arm, hip and leg bones show they were strong yet lightweight. Their shapes were not just suited for gliding, but probably also designed for powered, flapping flight. Whether all four limbs flapped at the same time, or just the arms, is not yet clear.

Survival tactics

Why fly? If Microraptor was mainly a tree-dweller, there are many reasons. These include crossing clearings and rivers, swooping onto prey, searching for a mate, and escaping the jaws of predators – including bigger theropods.

Can't catch me!

For many years Compsognathus, from 150 million years ago in Europe, held the record as the smallest dinosaur. But several even tinier kinds are now known, including Microraptor.

Killer claws

E specially famous among killer dinosaurs are the raptors – a name that means 'thief', 'grabber' or 'plunderer'. Officially, the group is known as dromaeosaurs, or 'running lizards'. However, many of them have 'raptor' in their name, such as Utahraptor, Microraptor, Velociraptor and Bambiraptor. Oddly, one of the most-studied dromaeosaurs does not have 'raptor' in its name. But its name does identify the group's key feature. This is Deinonychus, or 'terrible claw', named after its truly lethal killing weapon – the large, curved, sharp, movable claw on the second toe of each foot.

Fast 'n' furious

Deinonychus prowled North America during the Middle Cretaceous, 110 million years ago. It was not especially large at 3 m (10 ft) long, 70 kg (155 lb.) in weight, and as tall as a human. But its fossil skeleton shows that, like many raptors, it was fast, agile and athletic. It could run, leap, twist and turn at high speed.

Super-sharp

The raptor's hooked, pointed second claw was much larger than the others. Raptor footprint fossils in China show indents made by the other claws but not the second claw. When moving around, Deinonychus probably retracted the second claw so it wouldn't become dull by scraping against the ground.

Several Deinonychus fossils found with a large plant-eating dinosaur suggest they hunted as a pack.

Multi-weapon

The deadly claw was an excellent weapon and tool. Its toe joints were very flexible so it could slash around in a curve, maybe to tear holes in prey or jab at enemies. It may have pierced and held down prey while the killer tore off pieces with its teeth.

Deinonychus had sharp teeth, but they weren't very strong. It may have used them to gash and wound prey. It then would have followed its victims until they were weak and easier to eat.

Fascinating fact

In the 1960s and 1970s, fossil expert John Ostrom's brilliant description of Deinonychus changed people's views of dinosaurs. Far from being slow, clumsy and dim-witted, he showed some were speedy, powerful, nimble and probably intelligent, as we believe today.

Watery grave

Spinosaurus was named in 1915 from fossils found in Egypt. New, more complete finds support the claim that Spinosaurus was the greatest-ever predator to walk the Earth.

No killer dinosaur has yet been found that was greater in size and power than awesome Spinosaurus. It could have been over 15 m (50 ft) long and 15 tonnes in weight – perhaps twice as heavy as Tyrannosaurus. This makes Spinosaurus the largest theropod and therefore the biggest land meat-eater of all time. But recent scientific studies show it was also highly adapted for swimming too. It probably caught mainly water-dwelling prey, especially fish, and lurked to grab other dinosaurs coming to the water's edge for a drink.

How big was huge?

Experts agree 'Spino' lived 110 to 95 million years ago in North Africa – but they don't all agree on its weight. Size estimates depend on whether the skeleton is fleshed out as a slim, lightweight creature, or as stocky and muscular. 'Spino' might have tipped the scales at just 7–8 tonnes – or it could have been a mega-bulky 20 tonnes.

Going for a swim

Spinosaurus had many adaptations for moving in water: nostrils and eyes high on its snout, a long bendy neck, large paddling arms and hands, a slim body, small hips, back legs suited to kick rather than run, a long swishy tail, and many solid bones (not air-filled like most theropods).

I do like a nice fish dish.

Spinos and crocs

Spinosaurs such as Baryonyx and Spinosaurus itself had several killer features similar to today's fish-eating crocodile, the Asian gharial. These included a long, low snout with slim jaws, and groups of pointy, cone-shaped teeth with gaps between. Fish scales and bones found with Spinosaurus fossils also show it had a taste for fish suppers.

Could Spinosaurus hunt well on land as well as in the water? Probably, although it was rather front-heavy, so it may have used its arms as well as legs to move at speed.

Mystery of the sail

One amazing feature of Spinosaurus was its back sail of skin, held up by bony rods along its spine. Was it for body temperature control?

A colourful display for rivals or mates? A fish-like 'fin' for better swimming? As yet, no one really knows.

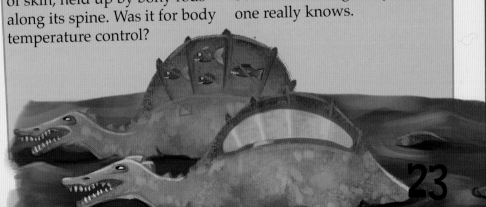

23

Land of the giants

What a big-head!

A distinct feature of Giganotosaurus was its truly enormous skull, up to 1.8 m (6 ft) long, with a large lower jaw bone or dentary. It could open its mouth very wide. Its teeth were not especially big, but plentiful, sharp and narrow, with saw-like edges for slicing and cutting.

Giganotosaurus, discovered in 1993, was the first meat-eating dinosaur for almost 100 years to be described as bigger than Tyrannosaurus. A massive and powerful theropod from the Middle-Late Cretaceous, 98 million years ago, it lurked among the woods, scrubland and swamps that once covered Argentina, South America. Even though its fossil skeleton was two-thirds complete, its unusual body proportions mean guesses of its size vary from a length of about 13 to 14 m (42 to 46 ft) long and a weight of 6 to 8 tonnes – slightly larger than Tyrannosaurus.

Argentina at this time was truly 'land of the giants'. Another theropod, only slightly smaller than 'Gig', was Mapusaurus. And massive sauropods included Argentinosaurus and Antarctosaurus.

Move over
T. rex!

24

The biggest meal?

Giganotosaurus prey may have included one of the most colossal creatures that ever lived. This was the sauropod Argentinosaurus, stretching more than 30 m (98 ft) from nose to tail and weighing perhaps 80 tonnes (88 tons). It lived around the same time as Giganotosaurus and also in the same region, as shown by its name.

Fascinating fact

In 1993, 'Gig' took the record from Tyrannosaurus as the biggest-ever killer dinosaur. However, it did not hold the title for long. New finds for Carcharodontosaurus and Spinosaurus soon indicated that they were even larger. In a few more years, who knows, maybe someone else will wear the crown?

Fast runner?

Fossil footprints or trackways in the same area as Giganotosaurus show each foot's mark was 50 cm (20 in) long, with prints about 130 cm (51 in) apart. Adding details of the leg's length and proportions, experts estimate it had a running speed of about 45 kilometres per hour (28 miles per hour) – slightly faster than a champion human sprinter.

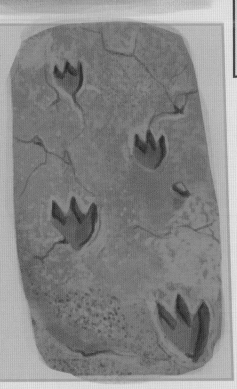

The first Giganotosaurus fossil was discovered when mechanic Ruben Carolini ran over it in his dune buggy! He is remembered in the killer's full name, Giganotosaurus carolinii.

Saw-toothed slayers

Carcharodontosaurus lived in the same region as Spinosaurus, though a few million years later. There were plenty of huge plant-eaters for these hunters, such as the sauropod Nigersaurus.

Great name!

Carcharodontosaurus means 'jagged-toothed lizard'. The name comes from the similarity of its teeth to those of another big hunter, the largest living predatory fish – the great white shark, Carcharodon.

All killer dinosaurs had big, sharp teeth. But these differed in the details of their design. One of the biggest theropods, enormous Carcharodontosaurus, dates back to 95 million years ago in North Africa. Its dagger-like teeth had especially noticeable tiny serrations along the front and rear edges. These serrations were not triangular, like the teeth of a saw blade. Instead, they were bumpy or wavy. This was a design similar to that of our steak knives, which are specially made for slicing flesh.

Second biggest killer?

The teeth of Carcharodontosaurus measured up to 23 cm (9 in) long. At up to 13 m (42 ft) in length and 9 to 10 tonnes in weight, this theropod may have just outsized Tyrannosaurus and Giganotosaurus. But it was probably not quite as immense as Spinosaurus.

Meaty slices

Clues from theropods similar to Carcharodontosaurus, such as Allosaurus, suggest how these mega-killers ate. They could have pulled the head back and forth and from side to side, using their teeth with a sawing motion to cut through flesh, gristle and even bone. This is different to how Tyrannosaurus used its teeth, which were able to crush bone.

The first fossils of Carcharodontosaurus (its teeth) were mistakenly identified as belonging to Megalosaurus.

Can you believe it?

Carcharodontosaurus fossils have been dug up in Morocco, Algeria and Egypt. These North African countries today are mostly desert – the vast Sahara. But 100 million years ago the area was green and lush, with rivers and lakes.

27

King of the killers

Everybody knows *my* name.

Famous for nearly a century as the biggest-ever land predator, Tyrannosaurus no longer holds that record. But it was still huge, at 12 m (39 ft) in length and weighing up to 10 tonnes (11 tons). It also remains one of the world's best-known creatures. The last of the mega-meat-eaters, Tyrannosaurus – often called *T. rex* – hunted around North America 66 million years ago, at the very end of the Cretaceous period. It may even have seen the giant space rock, or asteroid, that smashed into Earth and set off the mass extinction that devastated most dinosaurs and much of the life on our planet.

Banana teeth

Tyrannosaurus's teeth had tiny serrations but were not thin and blade-like. They were shaped like tall, slim, slightly curved cones, giving them the nickname 'stout bananas'. Rather than stabbing, slicing and carving, this design was more suited to tearing and crushing.

Bite power

Tyrannosaurus had almost the greatest bite power of any animal that ever existed. As well as having stout teeth, its skull and jaws were big with large surfaces for strong muscles. This can be seen in one of the best fossil specimens, known as 'Stan', which is more than two-thirds complete.

How fast could *T. rex* run? Estimates vary from a sluggish 20 kilometres per hour (12 mph), to a super-sprinting 60 kilometres per hour (37 mph)!

It's a hard life...

Hunter or scrounger?

Experts have long argued over whether Tyrannosaurus was an active hunter, chasing after prey, or a lazy scavenger feeding on any dead bodies it found. Being so big, maybe it chased away smaller predators and took over their kills. Or perhaps, like hyenas today, it used all of these tactics.

Did Tyrannosaurus live in families and hunt in packs? Some experts believe so, but there is little hard evidence. It's another Tyrannosaurus mystery waiting to be solved.

Survival tactics

Tyrannosaurus skulls studied in medical scanners reveal what's inside. The results show that this killer was an air-head! There were many air spaces and passages, especially in the nasal cavity used for smell. So sniffing out scents and odours was important.

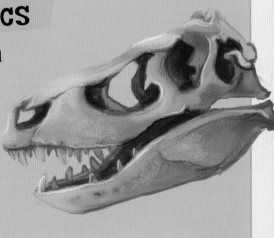

Glossary

Asteroid A large rock hurtling through space, usually hundreds to thousands of metres across.

Carnivory Adapted to eating mainly meat or meaty flesh.

Claws Hard endings to fingers and toes that usually taper to a point.

Cretaceous period A period in the Earth's history lasting from approximately 146 to 65 million years ago.

Evolve Develop gradually over many generations.

Fossil The remains of a prehistoric organism embedded in rock and preserved in a petrified (stony) form.

Jurassic period A period in the Earth's history lasting from approximately 201 to 145 million years ago.

Mass extinction When many kinds of living things die out forever in a short time, from a few years to a million or two million years.

Mesozoic era A span of prehistoric time that started 252 million years ago and ended 65 million years ago. It contained the Triassic, Jurassic and Cretaceous periods.

Moult To shed or get rid of a body covering and grow a new one, such as feathers in birds, fur in mammals or scales in reptiles.

Pack A group of animals living together, usually hunters who work together and cooperate to catch prey.

Palaeontologist An expert in fossil animals and plants.

Piscivory Adapted to eating mainly fish.

Predator A creature that hunts, catches and eats other animals, its prey.

Prey A creature that is caught and eaten by a hunting animal, a predator.

Quill The long, stiff, central part of a bird's feather.

Raptor A name that means 'thief', 'grabber' or 'plunderer', used for the group of dinosaurs called dromaeosaurs, and also for birds of prey such as hawks and eagles.

Recurved Hook-shaped and pointing backwards.

Reptile A cold-blooded vertebrate animal possessing dry, scaly skin, which typically lays soft-shelled eggs on land. Reptiles include snakes, lizards and crocodiles.

Sauropods Mostly very large plant-eating dinosaurs with a small head, long bendy neck and tail, and wide body with four stout legs. The name means 'lizard-feet'.

Scavenger A creature that feeds mainly on dead and dying animals.

Serrations A row of small, wavy, sharp or tooth-like projections, like on a saw or a steak knife.

Species A single kind or type of animal with a two-part official scientific name, such as *Tyrannosaurus rex*.

Theropods Dinosaurs that mostly specialised in hunting and killing prey, with sharp teeth and claws, and who walked on two back legs. The name means 'beast-feet'.

Trackways Rows or lines of footprints, pawprints or similar, either freshly made or preserved, that show how an animal moved.

Triassic period A period in the Earth's history lasting from approximately 252 to 201 million years ago.

Vanes Side-branches of a bird's feathers, that stick out from the central quill.

Vertebrate An animal that possesses a backbone.

Index